Life

Instruction Book
Volume II

Also available from HarperCollins

Life's Little Instruction Book
by H Jackson Brown, Jnr

The Lovers' Little Instruction Book
by Cindy Francis

A Gardener's Little Instruction Book
by Violet Wood

A Baby's Little Instruction Book
by David Brawn

Life's Little Instruction Book Volume II

H. Jackson Brown, Jnr

HarperCollinsPublishers

HarperCollins*Publishers*
77–85 Fulham Palace Road,
Hammersmith, London W6 8JB

First published in the UK by Thorsons 1993
This edition 2000

3 5 7 9 10 8 6 4 2

A catalogue record for this book
is available from the British Library

ISBN 0 00 710100 7

Printed and bound in Great Britain by
Martins the Printers Ltd, Berwick upon Tweed

Introduction

Life is a process. We are all works in progress – green tomatoes ripening on the windowsill of life. As I experience more, learn more, and contemplate more, I often think of what use my discoveries might be to my son, Adam.

Several years ago I jotted down a list of advice for him as he left home to begin college. At the time I thought the list was fairly complete.

But within a few days of presenting him with the 32 typed pages that became *Life's Little*

Instruction Book, I began to think of other entries I wished I had included. How could I have forgotten to mention 'Never be the first to break a family tradition', or 'Believe in love at first sight', or practical advice like 'Don't ride a bicycle barefoot' and 'Never drive while holding a cup of coffee between your knees?' Obviously there was only one thing to do – start another list. I promised myself I wouldn't send it to him until it reached at least 512 entries – one more than the original list. It took two years to complete.

The day Adam received it, he called from his apartment. 'Dad,' he said, 'this new list is terrific. I think it's more useful than the first one. Does this mean I should liik for a new volume of *Life's Little Instruction Book* every two years?'

'Would you like that?' I asked.

'Oh, yes,' he said.

'I'll see what I can do,' I replied, with not a small degree of satisfaction.

Little does Adam know that I can no more stop writing down these suggestions and observations than I could stop at a doughnut shop and order only coffee.

Life keeps coming at me, and new insights and discoveries get caught in my net. Like a fisherman, I haul them up, sort the catch, and head for the harbour. It's late and getting dark. But up ahead, standing on the dock, is a young man holding a lantern welcoming me. It's my son, Adam.

- Believe in love at first sight.
- Never laugh at anyone's dreams.
- Overpay good baby sitters.
- Love deeply and passionately. You might get hurt, but it's the only way to live life completely.

- Accept a breath mint if someone offers you one.

- Take along a small gift for the host or hostess when you're a dinner guest. A book is a good choice.

- Discipline with a gentle hand.

Talk slowly
but think quickly.

- Open the car door for you wife and always help her with her coat.

- If called for jury service, look on it positively. You'll learn a lot.

- When reconvening after a conference break, choose a chair in a different part of the room.

- Read the books shortlisted every year for the Booker Prize.

- Rake a big pile of leaves every autumn and jump in it with someone you love.

- Volunteer. Sometimes the jobs no one wants conceal big opportunities.

- Never drive while holding a cup of coffee between your knees.

- Carry a container of wet wipes in your glove compartment.

- Park in the end space in car parks. Your car door will have half the chance of getting dented.

- To dry wet shoes, stuff them with newspaper and let them dry naturally.

- Never miss an opportunity to ride a roller coaster.

- Don't let your family get so busy that you don't sit down to at least one meal a day together.

- Never miss an opportunity to sleep outside in hot weather.

- Sign all guarantee cards and send them in promptly.

- Drive as you wish your kids would. Never speed or drive recklessly with children in the car.

- Ask about a shop's return policy when you purchase an item that costs more than £50.
- Never be the first to break a family tradition.
- Never miss an opportunity to have someone rub your back.

- Keep a diary of your accomplishments at work. Then when you ask for a raise, you'll have the information you need to back it up.

- Have a professional photo of yourself made. Update it every three years.

- Don't judge people by their relatives.

- In disagreements, fight fairly. No name calling.

- Use a travel agent. It costs no more and saves time and effort.

- Remember that everyone you meet is afraid of something, loves something, and has lost something.

- When you go to borrow money, dress as if you have plenty of it.

- Never take the last piece of fried chicken.

- Check hotel bills carefully, especially the charges for local and long-distance calls.

- Eat a piece of chocolate to cure bad breath from onions or garlic.

- Never sign contracts with blank spaces.

- Remember the three Rs: Respect for self; Respect for others; Responsibility for all your actions.

- Put your address inside your luggage as well as on the outside.

- Don't admire people for their wealth but for the creative and generous ways they put it to use.

- Never pick up anything off the floor of a cab.

- Seize every opportunity for additional training in your job.
- When travelling, leave the good jewellery at home.
- Take along two big safety pins when you travel so that you can pin the curtains shut in your hotel room.

- When someone asks you a question and you don't want to answer, smile and ask, 'Why do you want to know?'

- Never give your credit card number over the phone unless you made the call and are sure who are you speaking to.

- Remember that just the moment you say, 'I give up,' someone else seeing the same situation is saying, 'My, what a great opportunity.'
- Never betray a confidence.
- Never leave the kitchen when something's boiling on the stove.

- Never claim a victory prematurely.
- Say 'bless you' when you hear someone sneeze.
- Make the punishment fit the crime.
- Keep the porch light on until all the family is in for the night.

- Remember that everyone is influenced by kindness.

- Never give anybody a fondue set or anything painted avocado green.

- Carry your own alarm clock when travelling. Hotel wake-up calls are sometimes unreliable.

- Pack a compass and a Swiss Army knife when hiking in unfamiliar territory.
- Never apologize for being early for an appointment.
- Plant courgettes only if you have lots of friends.

- Borrow a box of puppies for an afternoon and take them to visit the residents of a retirement home. Stand back and watch the smiles.

- When you lose, don't lose the lesson.

- When you feel terrific, notify your face.

- Don't be surprised to discover that luck favours those who are prepared.

- When lost or in distress, signal in 'threes' – three shouts, three gunshots, or three horn blasts.

- Never be photographed with a cocktail glass in your hand.

- Don't let a little dispute injure a great friendship.
- Don't marry anyone who picks at their food.
- When asked to play the piano, do it without complaining or making excuses.

- Create a little signal only your wife knows so that you can show her you love her across a crowded room.
- Read a book about beekeeping.
- Subscribe to *Which?* magazine.
- Carry a small pocket knife.

- Keep a well-stocked first-aid kit in your car and at home.
- Order a seed catalogue. Read it the day after the clocks go back.
- Every so often, invite the person behind you in the queue to go ahead of you.

- Don't overlook life's small joys while searching for the big ones.

- Look for ways to make your boss look good.

- When you have the choice of two exciting things, choose the one you haven't tried.

- Take off the conference badge as soon as you leave the venue.

- Remember that the person who steals an egg will steal a chicken.

- Meet regularly with someone who holds vastly different views from you.

Give people more than they expect and do it cheerfully.

- Remember that no time spent with your children is ever wasted.
- Don't go looking for trouble.
- Don't buy someone else's trouble.
- Don't expect your love alone to make a neat person out of a messy one.

- Be the first to fight for a just cause.

- Remember that no time is ever wasted that makes two people better friends.

- Check to see if your own car insurance covers you when you rent a car. The insurance offered by car rental companies is expensive.

- There are people who will always come up with reasons why you can't do what you want to do. Ignore them.

- Avoid approaching horses and restaurants from the rear.

- Never say anything uncomplimentary about another person's dog.

- If you need to bring in a business partner, make sure your partner brings along some money.

- Never miss a chance to dance with your wife.

- Don't ride in a car if the driver has been drinking.

- If you have trouble with a company's products or services, go to the top. Write to the managing director, then follow up with a phone call.

- Think twice before accepting the lowest bid.

- Don't judge what you don't understand.

- Pay your bills on time. If you can't, write your creditors a letter describing your situation. Send them something every month, even if it's only five pounds.

- When boarding a bus, say 'hello' to the driver. Say 'thank you' when you get off.

☼ When uncertain what to wear, a blue blazer, worn with grey wool slacks, a white shirt, and a red-and-blue striped silk tie, is almost always appropriate.

☼ When in doubt about what art to put on a wall, choose a framed black-and-white photo by Ansel Adams.

- Never give a gift that's not beautifully wrapped.

- When you realize you've made a mistake, take immediate steps to correct it.

- Don't think expensive equipment will make up for lack of talent or practice.

- Learn to say 'I love you' in French, Italian and Swedish.

- Own an umbrella big enough for two people to share without getting wet.

- Make allowances for your friends' imperfections as readily as you do for your own.

- Don't waste time trying to appreciate music you dislike. Spend the time with music you love.

- When you are totally exhausted but have to keep going, wash your face and hands and put on clean socks and a clean shirt. You will feel remarkably refreshed.

- Write a short note inside the front cover when giving a book as a gift.

- When concluding a business deal and the other person suggests working out the details later, say, 'I understand, but I would like to settle the entire matter right now.' Don't move from the table until you do.

- Make the rules for your children clear, fair and consistent.
- Be ruthlessly realistic when it comes to your finances.
- Do your homework and know your facts, but remember it's passion that persuades.

- Set high goals for your employees and help them attain them.

- Set aside your dreams for your children and help them attain their own dreams.

- Smile when picking up the phone. The caller will hear it in your voice.

- Ask anyone giving you directions to repeat them at least twice.

- Steer clear of any place with a 'Ladies Welcome' sign in the window.

- Be open and accessible. The next person you meet could become your best friend.

☼ Always put something in the collection plate.

- Ask yourself if you would feel comfortable giving your two best friends a key to your house. If not, look for some new best friends.

- Do the right thing, regardless of what others think.

- Buy the big bottle of Tabasco.

- Judge people from where they stand, not from where you stand.

- When shaking a woman's hand, squeeze it no harder than she squeezes yours.

- Never wash a car, mow a lawn, or select a Christmas tree after dark.

- Life will sometimes hand you a magical moment. Savour it.

- Don't give away the ending of good films and books.

- Learn to save on even the most modest salary. If you do, you're almost assured of financial success.

- Dress a little better than your clients but not as well as your boss.

- Take the stairs when it's four flights or less.

- Buy a used car with the same caution a naked man uses to climb a barbed-wire fence.

- Memorize your favourite love poem.
- Never threaten if you don't intend to back it up.
- Hold yourself to the highest standards.
- Be the first to forgive.

- Don't confuse comfort with happiness.

- Don't confuse wealth with success.

- Wear smart clothes to job interviews, even for a job stacking shelves.

- Don't cut corners.

- Whenever you take something back for an exchange or refund, wear a jacket and tie.

- Check the toilet paper *before* sitting down.

- Every year celebrate the day you and your partner had your first date.

- Don't knock the competition.

- Make a habit of reading something inspiring and cheerful just before going to sleep.

- Marry someone you love to talk to. As you get older, conversational skills will be as important as any other.

- If you work for an organization that makes its decisions by committee, make sure you're on the committee.
- When employing people, give special consideration to anyone who's gained a Duke of Edinburgh's Award.
- Spend some time alone.

- Never buy anything electrical at a market.

- Remember that a person who is foolish with money is foolish in other ways too.

- Everyone loves praise. Look hard for ways to give it to them.

- When talking to your doctor, don't let him or her interrupt or end the session early. It's your body. Stay until all your questions are answered to your satisfaction.

- Everyone deserves a birthday cake. Never celebrate a birthday without one.

- If you want to do something and you feel in your bones that it's the right thing to do, do it. Intuition is often as important as the facts.

- Be as friendly to the security guard as you are to the chairman of the board.

- Learn to bake bread.

- When it comes to worrying or painting a picture, know when to stop.

- Before taking a long trip, fill your tank and empty your bladder.

- Open your arms to change, but don't let go of your values.

- Be an original. If that means being a little eccentric, so be it.

- Pay as much attention to the things that are working positively in your life as you do to those that are giving you trouble.

- Give a poor child an Easter egg.

- Ask for double prints when you have film processed. Send the extras to the people in the photos.

- Treat your employees with the same respect you give your clients.

- Slow down. I mean *really* slow down when there's a school nearby.

Turn enemies into friends by doing something nice for them.

- When taking a woman home, make sure she's safely inside her house before you leave.

- You may be fortunate and make a lot of money. But be sure your work involves something that enriches your spirit as well as your bank account.

- Allow your children to face the consequences of their actions.
- Conduct yourself in such a way that your old school would want you to make a speech at Prizegiving.
- Don't expect the best gifts to come wrapped in pretty paper.

- Live with your new pet several days before you name it. The right name will come to you.

- When a good man or woman runs for political office, support him or her with your time and money.

- What you must do, do cheerfully.

- Remember that silence is sometimes the best answer.

- Don't dismiss a good idea simply because you don't like the source.

- Don't think you can relax your way to happiness. Happiness comes as a result of *doing*.

- Don't buy a cheap mattress.

- Don't expect anyone to know what you want for Christmas if you don't tell them.

- Don't waste time waiting for inspiration. Begin, and inspiration will find you.

- When you need professional advice, get it from professionals, not from your friends.

- Choose a church that sings joyful music.

- Don't believe all you hear, spend all you have, or sleep all you want.

- Win without boasting.
- Lose without excuses.
- Watch your attitude. It's the first thing people notice about you.
- Be engaged at least six months before you get married.
- Be quick to take advantage of an advantage.

- When you say, 'I love you,' mean it.
- When you say, 'I'm sorry,' look the person in the eye.
- Pack a light bathrobe on overnight trips. Take your pillow, too.
- Choose the top floor flat.

- Ask someone you'd like to know better to list five people he would most like to meet. It will tell you a lot about him.

- Don't be a person who says, 'Ready, fire, aim.'

- Don't be a person who says, 'Ready, aim, aim, aim.'

- Deadlines are important. Meet them.

- When you find someone doing small things well, put him or her in charge of bigger things.

- Remove your sunglasses when you talk to someone.

- Watch less TV.

- Remember that a good price is not necessarily what an object is marked, but what it is worth to you.

- When a friend or loved one becomes ill, remember that hope and positive thinking are strong medicines.

- Remember that the more you know, the less you fear.

- When a waitress or waiter provides exceptional service, leave a generous tip, plus a short note like, 'Thanks for the wonderful service.'

- Read more books.

- Buy three best-selling children's books. Read them and then give them to a youngster.
- Introduce yourself to your neighbours as soon as you move into a new area.
- Be your children's best teacher and coach.

When opportunity knocks, invite it to stay for dinner.

- When you find something you really want, don't let a few pounds keep you from getting it.

- Don't confuse mere inconveniences with real problems.

- Strive for perfection, but settle for excellence.

- Some things need doing better than they've ever been done before. Some just need doing. Others don't need doing at all. Know which is which.

- When travelling by plane, don't pack valuables or important papers in your suitcase. Carry them on board with you.

- Show extra respect for people whose jobs put dirt under their fingernails.
- Don't do business with anyone who has a history of suing people.
- Hold your child's hand as often as you can. The time will come all too soon when he or she won't let you.

- When you carve the Christmas turkey, give the first piece to the person who prepared it.

- Live a good, honourable life. Then when you get older and think back, you'll enjoy it a second time.

- Learn to juggle.

- Purchase one piece of original art each year, even if it's just a small oil painting by a student.
- Volunteer to help a few hours a month working in a soup kitchen.
- Wipe the sticky honey jar before putting it back on the shelf.

- Don't think people at the top of their professions have all the answers. They don't.

- Learn to make great spaghetti sauce.

- If you treated unfairly by an airline, contact the Air Transport Users' Committee on 020 7242 3882.

- Get a car with a sun roof.

- Don't carry expensive luggage. It's a tip off to thieves that expensive items may be inside.

- Buy ladders, extension cords and garden hoses longer than you think you'll need.

- Be humble and polite, but don't let anyone push you around.

- Put your jacket around your girlfriend on a chilly evening.

- Once every couple of months enjoy a four-course meal – but eat each course at a different restaurant.

- Introduce yourself to someone you would like to meet by smiling and saying, 'My name is Adam Brown. I haven't had the pleasure of meeting you.'

- Be advised that when negotiating, if you don't get it in writing, you probably won't get it.

- Wrap a couple of thick rubber bands around your wallet when you're fishing or hiking. This will prevent it from slipping out of your pocket.

- Do 100 push-ups every day: 50 in the morning and 50 in the evening.

- Keep your private thoughts private.

- Put the strap around your neck before looking through binoculars.

- Don't expect bankers to come to your aid in a crisis.

- Every so often let your spirit of adventure triumph over your good sense.

- Remember that a good example is the best sermon.

- Wear goggles when operating a power saw or drill.

- Use a favourite picture of a loved one as a bookmark.

- Before going to bed on Christmas Eve, join hands with your family and sing 'Silent Night'.

- Surprise an old friend with a phone call.

- Get involved at your child's school.

- Champion your spouse. Be his or her best friend and biggest fan.

- Don't accept unacceptable behaviour.

- Carry a list of your spouse's important measurements in your wallet.

- Add to your children's private library by giving them a hardback copy of one of the classics every birthday. Begin with their first birthday.

- Read between the lines.

- Don't say no until you've heard the whole story.

- When you are a dinner guest, take a second helping if it's offered, but never a third.

- Write your favourite author a note of appreciation.

- Never lose your nerve, your temper, or your car keys.

- Don't open credit card bills at the weekend.

- Never start the car until all passengers have fastened their seat belts.

- Never say anything uncomplimentary about your wife or children in the presence of others.

- Send your mother-in-law flowers on your wife's birthday.

- Use your past successes as a trampoline, not as an easy chair.

- When eating at a restaurant that features foreign food, don't order anything you could make at home.

- Apologize immediately when you lose your temper, especially to children.

- Buy your fiancée the nicest diamond engagement ring you can afford.

- When you're uncertain of what you should pay someone, ask, 'What do you think is fair?' You'll almost always get a reasonable answer.

- Be wary of the man who's 'all hat and no cattle'.

- Read Thoreau's *Walden*.

Trust in God
but lock your car.

- When giving a speech, concentrate on what you can give the audience, not what you can get from them.

- Don't be so concerned with your rights that you forget your manners.

- Remember that almost everything looks better after a good night's sleep.

☼ A loving atmosphere in your home is so important. Do all you can to create a tranquil, harmonious home.

☼ Use a camcorder to videotape the contents of your home for insurance purposes. Don't forget cupboards and drawers. Keep the tape in your bank safe-deposit box.

- When you know that someone has gone to a lot of trouble to get dressed up, tell them they look terrific!

- Avoid using the word *impacted* unless you are describing wisdom teeth.

- Keep a separate shaving kit packed for travelling.

- Stop and watch a farmer ploughing a field.

- When you tell a child to do something, don't follow it with, 'Okay?' Ask instead, 'Do you understand?'

- Spend a day at the races.

- When you see visitors taking pictures of each other, offer to take a picture of their group together.

- Mind the store. No one cares about your business the way you do.

- Get to car boot sales early. The good stuff is usually gone by 8.00 a.m.

- Stop and watch stonemasons at work.

- Choose a subject you know nothing about and start trying to learn all you can about it.

- In disagreements with loved ones, deal with the current situation. Don't bring up the past.

- Every so often watch *Blue Peter*.

- Remember that *how* you say something is as important as *what* you say.

- Never apologize for extreme measures when defending your values, your health or your family's safety.

Don't let weeds grow around your dreams.

- Don't think you can fill an emptiness in your heart with money.

- Become famous for finishing important, difficult tasks.

- Never sell your teddy bear, school scarf or favourite childhood books. You'll regret it later.

- Leave a small coin where a child can find it.

- Clean out a different drawer in your house every week.

- Do a good job because you want to, not because you have to. This puts you in charge instead of your boss.

- Buy a new tie to wear to your wedding. Wear it only once. Keep it forever.

- When you're lost, admit it, and ask for directions.

- Never type a love letter. Use a fountain pen.

- Place a note reading 'Your licence number has been reported to the police' on the windshield of a car illegally parked in a disabled space.

- Remember that the shortest way to get anywhere is to have good company travelling with you.

- Never buy just one roll of toilet paper, one roll of film or one jar of peanut butter. Get two.

- Never buy a chair or sofa without first sitting on it for several minutes.

- At the end of your days, be leaning forward – not falling backwards.

- Don't be thin-skinned. Take criticism as well as praise with equal grace.

- Never eat liver at a restaurant. Some things should be done only in the privacy of one's home.

- Share your knowledge. It's a way to achieve immortality.

Don't take good friends, good health or a good marriage for granted.

- Keep impeccable tax records.
- Help a child plant a small garden.
- Don't work for a company led by someone of questionable character.
- Spend your time and energy creating, not criticizing.

- Read bulletin boards at the supermarket, college bookshop and launderette. You will find all sorts of interesting things there.

- The next time you meet a police officer, fireworker or ambulance worker, tell them that you appreciate what they do.

- Act with courtesy and fairness regardless of how others treat you. Don't let them determine your response.

- When working with contractors, include a penalty clause in your contract for their not finishing on time.

- Visit your old school and introduce yourself to the head. Ask if you can sit in on a couple of classes.

- Respect sailing boats, snowmobiles and motorcycles. They can teach you a painful lesson very fast.

- Challenge yourself. Aim high.

- In a verbal confrontation, lower your voice to the degree that the other person raises his or hers.

- Let your children see you do things for your wife that lets them know how much you love and treasure her.

- Don't leave hair in the shower drain.

- Learn three knock-knock jokes so you will always be ready to entertain children.

- When you are a dinner guest at a restaurant, don't order anything more expensive than your host does.

- Don't outlive your money.

- Take photographs of every car you own. Later, these photos will trigger wonderful memories.

- Remember that nothing really important ever happens until someone takes a chance.

- Never grab at a falling knife.

- Think twice before deciding not to charge for your work. People often don't value what they don't pay for.

- When someone offers to pay you now or later, choose now.

- Don't take nine items to the eight items or less queue.

- Never take what you can't use.
- When there is a hill to climb, don't think that waiting will make it smaller.
- When your dog dies, frame its collar and put it above a window facing west.

- When a garment label warns 'Dry Clean Only', believe it.

- Beware the life empty of ambitions.

- Write the date and the names of non-family members on the backs of all photos as soon as you get them back from the developer.

Be gentle
with the Earth.

- Read a lot when you're on vacation, but nothing that has to do with your business.

- Start every day with the most important thing you have to do. Save the less important tasks for later.

- Mind your own business.

- At meetings, resist turning around to see who has just arrived late.
- Don't ride a bicycle or motorcycle barefooted.
- Refuse to share personal and financial information unless you feel it is absolutely essential.

Just because you earn a decent wage, don't look down on those who don't. To put things in perspective, consider what would happen to the public good if you didn't do your job for 30 days. Next, consider the consequences if sanitation workers didn't do their jobs for 30 days. Now, whose job is more important?

- Don't purchase anything in a package that appears to have been opened.

- Be willing to lower your price in order to get something else of greater value.

- Remember that what's right isn't always popular, and what's popular isn't always right.

Pray. There is immeasurable power in it.

- Call a nursing home or retirement centre and ask for a list of the residents who seldom get mail or visitors. Send them a card several times a year. Sign it, 'Someone who thinks you are very special.'

- Schedule your stag night at least two days before your wedding.

- Before buying a house or renting a flat, check the water pressure by turning on the taps and the shower and then flushing the toilet.

- Don't do business with people who knock on your door and say, 'I just happened to be in the neighbourhood.'

- Properly fitting shoes should feel good as soon as you try them on. Don't believe the salesperson who says, 'They'll be fine as soon as you break them in.'

- When making toast, don't put the knife back in the butter after you've put it in the marmalade.

- Overestimate travel time by 15 per cent.

- Choose a business partner the way you choose a tennis partner. Select someone who's strong where you are weak.

- Make duplicates of all important keys.

- Get your hair cut a week before the big interview.

- Spend your life lifting people up, not putting them down.

- Don't trust a woman or man who doesn't close their eyes when you kiss them.

- Never interrupt when you are being flattered.

- Never tell a person who's experiencing deep sorrow, 'I know how you feel.' You don't.

- In business or in life, don't follow the wagon tracks too closely.

- Own a comfortable chair for reading.

- Own a set of good kitchen knives.

- Own a stylish hat.

- Don't call a fishing rod a 'pole', a line a 'rope', a rifle a 'gun' or a ship a 'boat'.

- Brush your teeth before putting on your tie.
- Never risk what you can't afford to lose.
- Keep candles and matches in the kitchen and bedroom in case of power failure.

Remember that great love and great achievements involve great risk.

- Never tell a man he's losing his hair. He already knows.

- Learn to use a needle and thread, a steam iron, and an espresso machine.

- Display your street number prominently on your house in case emergency vehicles need to find you.

- Never say, 'My child would never do that.'

- Once a year, go somewhere you've never been before.

- Remember that what you give will afford you more pleasure than what you get.

- For peace of mind, make decisions in concert with your values.

- Remember that ignorance is expensive.

- If you make a lot of money, put it to use helping others while you are living. That is wealth's greatest satisfaction.

- Get your name off mailing lists by writing to: Mailing Preference Service, Freepost 22, London W1E 7EZ, with your name, address and postcode.

- Listen to your critics. They will keep you focused and innovative.

- Never say anything to a news reporter that you don't want to see on the front page of your local paper. Comments made 'off the record' seldom are.

- Remember that not getting what you want is sometimes a stroke of good luck.

- Don't pick up after your children. That's their job.

- Remember the old proverb, 'Out of debt, out of danger.'

- When someone has provided you with exceptional service, write a note to his or her boss.

- When declaring your rights, don't forget your responsibilities.

- Replace the batteries in smoke alarms every January 1st.

- Never ask an accountant, lawyer or doctor professional questions in a social setting.

- Perform your job better than anyone else can. That's the best job security.

- Remember that everyone you meet wears an invisible sign. It reads 'Notice me. Make me feel important.'

- Never employ someone you wouldn't invite home to dinner.

- Think twice before accepting a job that requires you to work in an office with no windows.

- When camping or hiking, never leave evidence that you were there.

- Dress respectfully when attending church.

- Remember that your child's character is like good soup. Both are homemade.

- Don't allow your dog to bark and disturb the neighbours.

- For easier reading in hotel rooms, pack your own 100-watt lightbulb.

- If you've learned that a good friend is ill, don't ask him about it. Let him tell you first.

- If you lend someone money, make sure his character exceeds the collateral.

- Go to air displays.

- Be cautious telling people how contented and happy you are. Many will resent it.

- Hang up if someone puts you on hold to take a 'call waiting'.

- Put love notes in your child's lunch box.

- Every once in a while ask yourself that question, If money weren't a consideration, what would I like to be doing?

- Remember that the best relationship is one where your love for each other is greater than your need for each other.

Learn the rules.
Then break some.

- Remember that half the joy of achievement is in the anticipation.

- Accept the fact that regardless of how many times you are right, you will sometimes be wrong.

- Whether it's life or a horse that throws you, get right back on.

- No matter how old you get, hug and kiss your mother whenever you greet her.

- Encourage anyone who is trying to improve mentally, physically or spiritually.

- Go to charity cricket matches.

- Go to barbecues.
- Order a charity Christmas catalogue.
- Keep in touch with your childhood friends – you have a lot of shared past.
- Help your children set up their own savings accounts by the age of 16.

- Get involved with your local government. As someone said, 'Politics is too important to be left to the politicians.'

- When trying on new clothes, take your wallet with you when you leave the changing room to look in the mirror.

- Never swap your integrity for money, power or fame.
- Never tell an off-colour joke when people of a different generation are present.
- Learn to play 'Happy Birthday' on the piano.

- Never sell yourself short.
- Never remind someone of a kindness or act of generosity you have shown him or her. Bestow a favour and then forget it.
- Put on old clothes before you get out the paint brushes.

- Fool someone on April 1st.
- When you need assistance, ask this way: 'I've got a problem. I wonder if you would be kind enough to help me?'
- When you get really angry, stick your hands in your pockets.

- Never be ashamed of honest tears.
- Never be ashamed of laughter that's too loud or singing that's too joyful.
- Never be ashamed of your patriotism.
- Don't trust your memory; write it down.

- Always try the house salad dressing.
- If your child's teacher is particularly good, tell the head.
- At least once, date someone with beautiful red hair.
- Watch the film *Regarding Henry*.

- Watch the film *Mr Smith Goes to Washington*.

- Visit friends and relatives when they are in hospital. You only need to stay a few minutes.

- Never leave a youngster in the car without taking the car keys.

- Don't think that sending a gift of flowers substitutes for your presence.

- When visiting a small town at lunch time, choose the café on the square.

- Attach a small Christmas wreath to your car's grill on the first day of December.

- Never ask a barber if you need a haircut.

- Truth is serious business. When criticizing others, remember that a little goes a long way.

- Don't confuse foolishness with bravery.

- When your children are learning to play musical instruments, buy them good ones.

- Don't discuss domestic problems at work.

- Never 'borrow' so much as a pencil from your workplace.

Judge your success by what you had to give up in order to get it.

- Never buy a piece of jewellery that costs more than £100 without doing a little haggling.

- Travel. See new places, but remember to take along an open mind.

- Be especially courteous and patient with older people.

- Become a tourist for a day in your own home town. Take a tour. See the sights.

- A racehorse that consistently runs just a second faster than another horse is worth millions of dollars more. Be willing to give that extra effort that separates the winner from the one in second place.

- Create a smoke-free office and home.

- Never eat a sugared doughnut when wearing a dark suit.

- Remember this statement by Coach Lou Holtz, 'Life is 10 per cent what happens to me and 90 per cent how I react to it.'

- Answer the easy questions first.
- Never ignore evil.
- Don't mistake kindness for weakness.
- Never get a tattoo.
- Let some things remain mysterious.

- Call before dropping in on friends and family.
- When you are away from home and hear church bells, think of someone who loves you.
- Every now and then, bite off more than you can chew.

- Never decide to do nothing just because you can only do a little. Do what you can.

- Acknowledge a gift, no matter how small.

- Remember that your character is your destiny.

- Let your handshake be as binding as a signed contract.

- Keep and file the best business letters you receive.

- Grind it out. Hanging on just one second longer than your competition makes you the winner.

- Buy and use your customers' products.

- Be better prepared than you think you will need to be.

- Buy a small, inexpensive camera. Take it with you everywhere.

- When friends offer to help, let them.

Approach love and cooking with reckless abandon.

- Pay the extra £5 for the best seats at a play or concert.

- Buy a red umbrella. It's easier to find among all the black ones, and it adds a little colour to rainy days.

- Employ people more for their judgement than for their talents.

- Every week, write a short poem.
- Worry makes for a hard pillow. When something's troubling you, before going to sleep, jot down three things you can do the next day to help solve the problem.
- Love someone who doesn't deserve it.

- Never buy anything from a rude salesperson, no matter how much you want it.

- Give handout materials after your presentation, never before.

- Every so often, go where you can hear seagulls crying.

- When you mean no, say it in a way that's not ambiguous.
- Attend a local fair or gala and support your community.
- When you're buying something that you only need to buy once, buy the best you can afford.

- Never open a restaurant.

- Give children toys that are powered by their imagination, not by batteries.

- Choose a seat in the row next to the emergency exit when flying. You will get more leg room.

- Reject and condemn prejudice based on race, gender, religion or age.

- As soon as you get married, start saving for your children's education.

- Read a magazine every week that has nothing to do with your hobbies or work.

- You may dress unconventionally, but remember that the more strangely you dress, the better you have to be.

- Be suspicious of a boss who schedules meetings instead of making decisions.

- Carry three business cards in your wallet.

Life is short.
Eat more pancakes and fewer rice cakes.

- Give the price of a night out to Shelter.

- Don't overfeed horses or brothers-in-law.

- For emergencies, always have a 50 pence piece in your pocket and a five pound note hidden in your wallet.

- Regardless of the situation, react with class.
- Buy raffle tickets, sweets and baked goods from pupils who are raising money for school projects.
- Become the kind person who brightens a room just by entering it.

- Remember the observation of William James that the deepest principle in human nature is the craving to be appreciated.

- When there's a piano to be moved, don't reach for the stool.

- Root for the home team.

- Go on blind dates. Remember, that's how I met your mother.

- Someone will always be looking at you as an example of how to behave. Don't let them down.

- Remember that the 'suggested retail price' seldom is.

- Follow your own star.
- Remember the ones who love you.
- Go home for the holidays.
- Don't get too big for your boots.
- Call your dad.

Dear Reader,

If you received advice from your parents or grandparents that was especially meaningful and you would like me to share it with other readers, please write and tell me about it.

I look forward to hearing from you.

H. Jackson Brown, Jr.
c/o Thorsons
77–85 Fulham Palace Road
Hammersmith
LONDON W6 8JB